™

The Polar Seas Encyclopedia Coloring Book

written and illustrated by Julia Pinkham

Stemmer House
PUBLISHERS, INC.

Introduction

The North and South Poles are vast, desolate regions covered in ice. The poles are colder than the rest of the world because they receive so much less of the sun's energy. This is due partly to the angle of the sun's rays as they strike the earth's surface, and also because the Polar ice fields reflect the sun's energy back into space like giant mirrors. During the long Polar winter, the sun stays below the horizon for six months, and the Polar Regions receive almost no sunlight at all.

Although they store most of the earth's water as ice, the Poles are actually deserts. Fresh water is extremely scarce, especially on Antarctica, where average temperatures never rise above freezing. Penguins have adapted to this lack of fresh water with a special gland that excretes the salt they ingest from drinking seawater.

The Arctic is actually an ocean covered in ice and ringed by land. For this reason, the Arctic does not get as cold as the Antarctic, which is an ice-covered continent surrounded by ocean. In the Arctic winter, temperatures may reach 60 degrees below zero, but during the short Arctic summer some areas reach 60 degrees above, allowing many life forms to flourish there, on land and in the sea.

2

The continent of Antarctica is the coldest, most inhospitable place on earth, with temperatures that reach 140 degrees below zero. Winds up to 200 miles an hour are not uncommon. There are no native peoples or any land animals living there, other than a few mites and small insects. But the oceans surrounding Antarctica are warmer, at around freezing, and they are teeming with life.

Because of the deep current upwellings, the cold Polar seas are rich with nutrients. Intense summer sunlight causes huge algal plankton blooms to occur. The plankton are food for huge masses of zooplankton, made up of many tiny animals such as fish, jellyfish, krill and the free-swimming larvae of bottom-dwelling creatures like sea stars, barnacles, hydroids and worms. Many species of birds, fishes and whales migrate to the Poles in the summer months to take advantage of this superabundance of food, departing again in winter when the sea ice begins to form again.

In spite of the harsh conditions, the Polar seas are among the richest environments on the planet. Some of the largest and rarest animals in the world depend on them for their continued existence, and so protection for the Polar Regions is as important as for the rainforests and other threatened environments of Earth.

J.P.

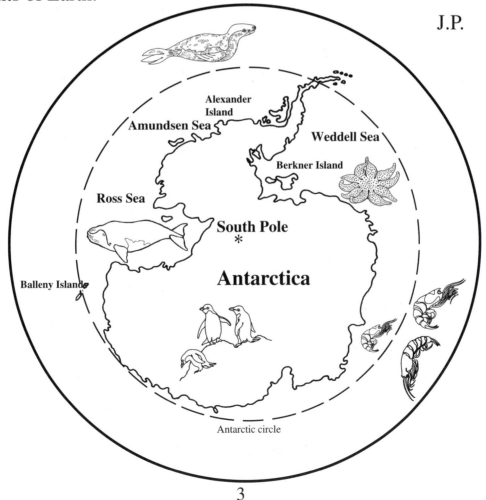

3

A

Adèlie penguins are black and white. Like all penguins, they are found only in the Southern hemisphere. Instead of wings, penguins have flippers. They cannot fly, but are excellent swimmers and can easily outswim a seal in open water. Penguins sometimes "porpoise" out of the water while swimming. They are the most vulnerable to waiting predators when they enter the water.

Anemones look like flowers, but they are actually animals. Their sticky red or green tentacles capture any small animals the ocean currents bring by, carrying them to the mouth in the center. Anemones grow to five inches.

Arctic terns migrate from the North Pole to the South Pole every year. In the fall, after the breeding season is over, they leave the northern Polar Regions and migrate to the Antarctic. This is one of the longest migrations made by any animal. Arctic terns spend seven months of the year flying.
While in the Antarctic they molt, spending several weeks barely able to fly. They live on the sea ice and feed on krill, which is abundant and easily caught. Arctic terns live many years, and may make the 10,000 mile journey from Pole to Pole twenty times or more. They always return to the same nesting site. Arctic terns are mainly white and grey, with black heads. Their beaks and feet are bright red.

B

Beluga whales, also called white whales because of their color, live in the Arctic year-round. They grow to just fifteen feet in length. Belugas have no dorsal fin. They are able to tolerate fresh water, and they gather in huge herds in warm shallow river estuaries in the summer. They rub their bodies on the gravel beds while they molt their skins. Their main enemy is the killer whale.

Baltic macoma clams live in mud or sand in bays and estuaries in the Arctic. They are white and brown and grow to one and one half inches.

Blue mussels are common bivalves that live in dense masses on rocks between the high and low tide lines in the Arctic and Pacific. They are a dark blue-black color with a brown foot.

Boreal astarte clams grow to two inches in length. Their shells are white and brown. Their Arctic range is circumpolar, and they live in mud, sand or gravel bottoms to 600 feet deep.

Bowhead whales are one of the few kinds of whale that live year-round in the Arctic. They are among the most endangered whales, owing to overhunting. Because bowheads sometimes use their huge heads to break breathing holes through the ice, beluga whales often follow them during winter. Bowheads are baleen whales, obtaining food by filtering krill and plankton from the water. They are blue-black.

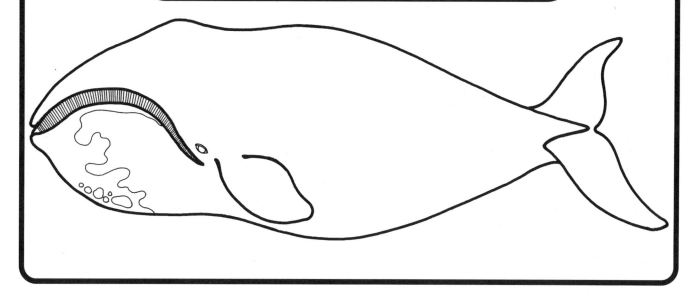

Bushy-backed sea slugs feed on hydroids. They are rusty-red or grey-brown in color. They live in and around kelp beds. Sea slugs are mollusks, related to the common garden slug or snail.

7

C **Chinstrap penguins** get their name from the thin black line that runs under their necks. They are black-and-white with yellow-brown eyes and a black beak. These penguins, which mate for life, nest in the summer on rocks on the islands of the Antarctic peninsula. They have thick, oily feather-down underneath their dense outer feathers, keeping them warm and dry in the coldest conditions. They also have a thick layer of fat, like seals, for protection from the cold.

Chink snails feed on seaweed. They live in eelgrass and kelp beds in the Arctic region. They are a quarter-inch long, and their shells are brown with yellow bands. The snail's head and foot are dark grey.

Chitons cling to rocks with their large foot. They scrape algae from rock surfaces with a mouth like a rasp. The white chiton is pale tan and a half-inch long. It is found in the Arctic and Pacific waters.

Crab-eater seals eat krill. Because their food is so plentiful, they are one of the most numerous seals found in the Antarctic. They have unusual interlocking teeth that strain krill from the seawater. Crab-eater pups are born with a complete set of teeth, and do not nurse for very long before they are on their own and able to fend for themselves. They live out on the open pack ice, sleeping and resting on ice floes. Their fur is a silvery-tan color.

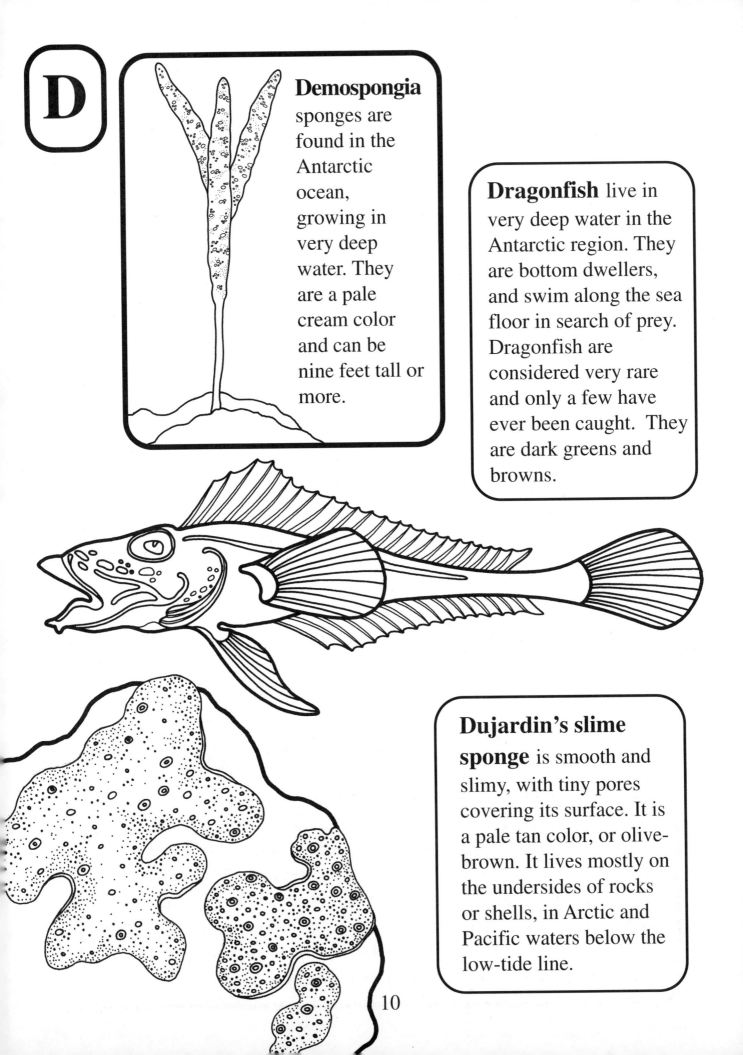

D

Demospongia sponges are found in the Antarctic ocean, growing in very deep water. They are a pale cream color and can be nine feet tall or more.

Dragonfish live in very deep water in the Antarctic region. They are bottom dwellers, and swim along the sea floor in search of prey. Dragonfish are considered very rare and only a few have ever been caught. They are dark greens and browns.

Dujardin's slime sponge is smooth and slimy, with tiny pores covering its surface. It is a pale tan color, or olive-brown. It lives mostly on the undersides of rocks or shells, in Arctic and Pacific waters below the low-tide line.

10

Duvaucelia are nudibranchs that are found in the Antarctic. Nudibranchs are shell-less sea slugs. They are predatory, feeding on hydroids and sponges. They are white or grey.

Dwarf brittle stars live entwined in kelp holdfasts, and in areas of sand or gravel under rocks in the Arctic and Pacific Oceans. They are quite brittle, but they can regenerate lost legs in just a few days. Brittle stars are bioluminescent, and glow a bright reddish-orange when excited. They move by writhing their long snaky legs. These sea stars brood their young in little pockets in the bases of their arms, where they develop into tiny brittle stars. They are gray, orange, red-orange or brown.

E

Emperor penguins are the largest of all the penguins, reaching a height of four feet. They are black and white, with bright yellow-orange and red marking on their necks, and an orange patch on the beak. Penguins are clumsy on land, but are swift and graceful swimmers. They hunt for squid and krill in large packs of fifty or more penguins. Their main enemies are leopard seals and killer whales. Emperor penguins breed during winter. After the eggs are laid, the females return to the sea to feed. Each bird lays a single egg. The male birds remain, huddling together to stay warm, holding the egg on their feet under a special fold of skin. The females return when the eggs are ready to hatch. If a chick hatches before the female returns with food, the male penguin provides a liquid food called "penguin's milk."

Elephant seals are the largest of the seals, the males reaching 8,000 pounds and twenty feet in length. They are grey-brown and tan. The elephant seal bulls use their large noses to make resonating sounds and loud bellows during the mating season, to frighten away rivals and attract females. They are usually solitary animals, except during the breeding season, when they gather in large colonies on beaches in the subantarctic islands.

F

Fin whales are the second largest whales in the world, reaching lengths of more than eighty feet. They are exceeded in length only by their close relatives, the giant blue whales, which grow to 100 feet long. Fin whales migrate to the Poles during the summer months to feed on krill, squid and schools of small fish. Adult fin whales can eat three tons of food a day. They are filter feeders, straining their food out of the water with the huge baleen plates that grow down from the roof of the mouth. The grooves in the throat allow it to expand during feeding. They are dark grey to brown, with white baleen plates on the left side of their heads.

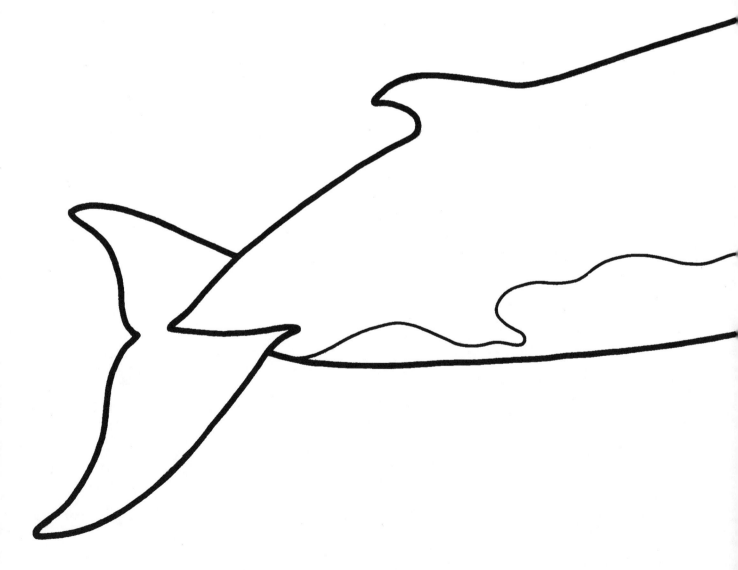

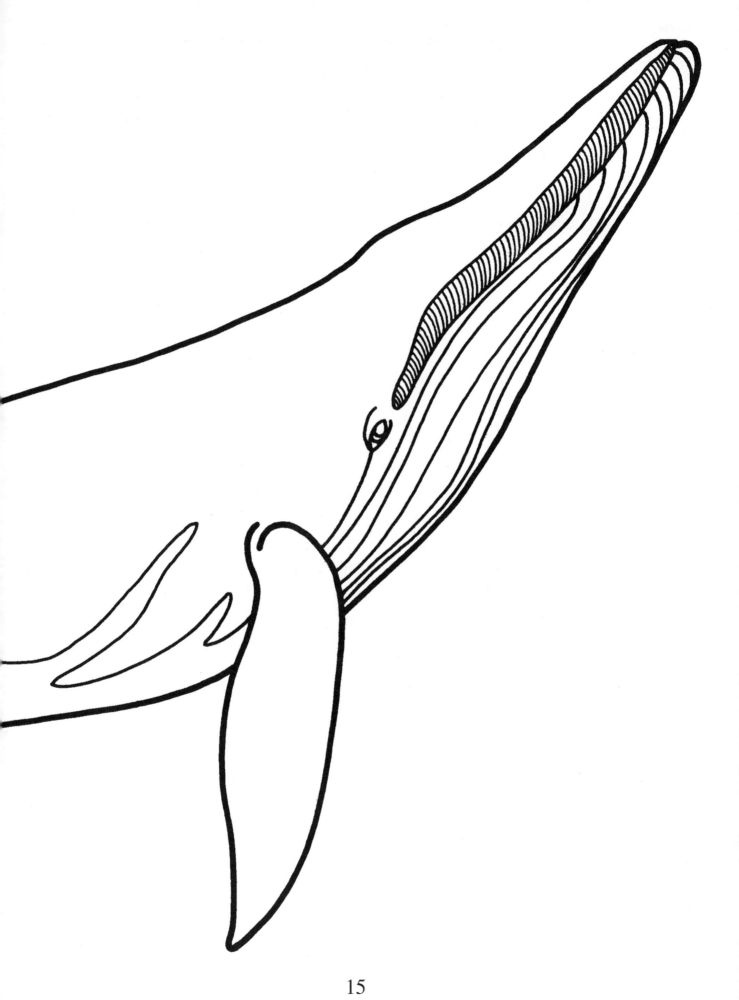

15

G

Greenland sharks grow up to twenty feet in length. They are the largest species of dogfish shark. They live in Arctic waters, often at great depths. They are sometimes seen at the surface, and they feed mainly on squid, seals, seabirds and, occasionally, porpoises or whales. They are grey.

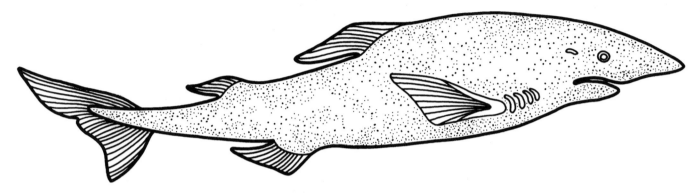

Goose neck barnacles are crustaceans. As larvae they are free-swimming plankton, but as adults they attach themselves permanently to kelp and other objects. They are often found washed ashore in the Arctic and Pacific coastal regions. They are brown and grey or white.

Green sponges are found in the Antarctic ocean. Sponges are the most common undersea life forms in the Polar Regions. Sponges come in many different shapes and sizes, from the hard encrusting types that look like cake frosting, to tall spires, vases and cylinders. Sponges are made up of a colony of cells, each with a specific function.

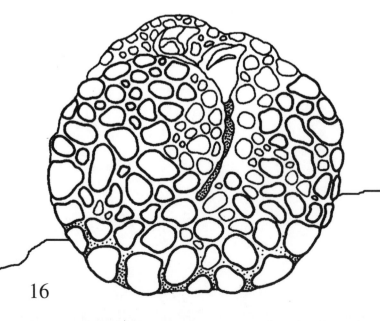

16

H

Hairy hermit crabs are covered with long reddish-brown bristles. They are found in both rocky tidepools and deep water in the Arctic and Pacific oceans. Hermit crabs must exchange shells for new ones as they grow. The larger hairy hermit crabs show a preference for the shells of whelks.

Hairy Doris are small lemon-yellow or purple-brown sea slugs found in the Arctic. They live among kelp and seaweeds, and feed on bryozoans.

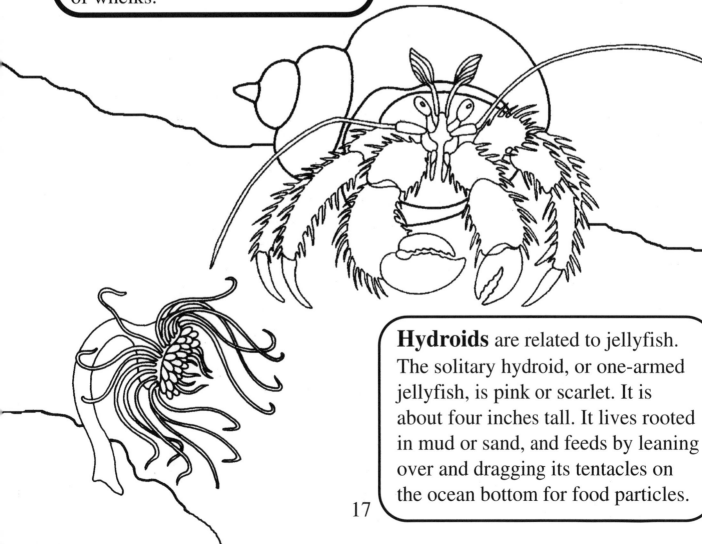

Hydroids are related to jellyfish. The solitary hydroid, or one-armed jellyfish, is pink or scarlet. It is about four inches tall. It lives rooted in mud or sand, and feeds by leaning over and dragging its tentacles on the ocean bottom for food particles.

17

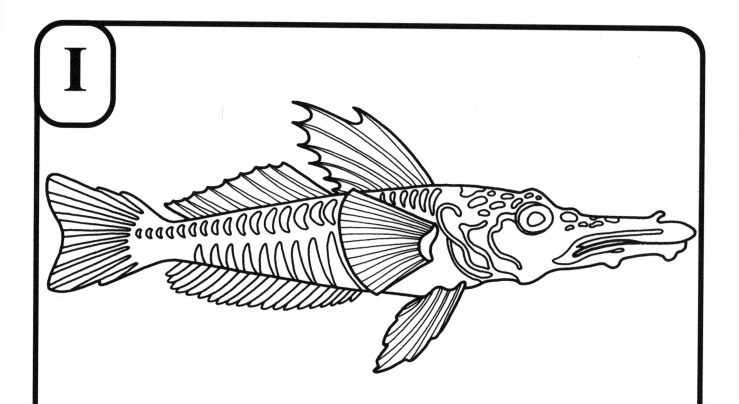

Ice fish are found only in the Antarctic ocean. They are an unusual clear purple color. Icefish are one of the only vertebrates without any red blood cells. Their blood is clear, or white. Oxygen is carried in their blood by plasma instead of red blood cells. This adaptation helps them survive in freezing temperatures, but they tend to be rather sluggish swimmers. They live on the ocean bottom, feeding on the numerous small invertebrates, worms and isopods that live there.

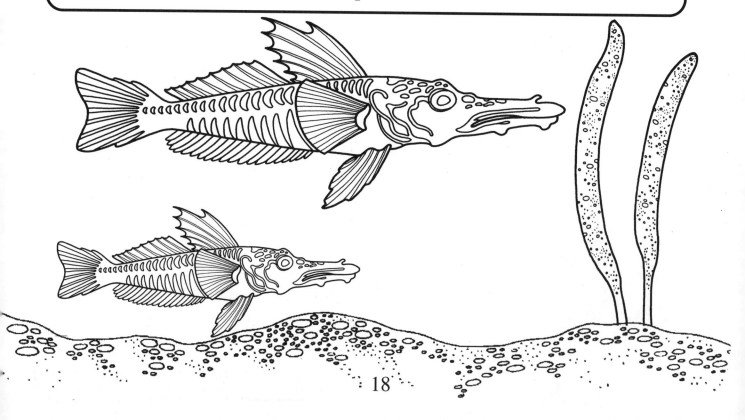

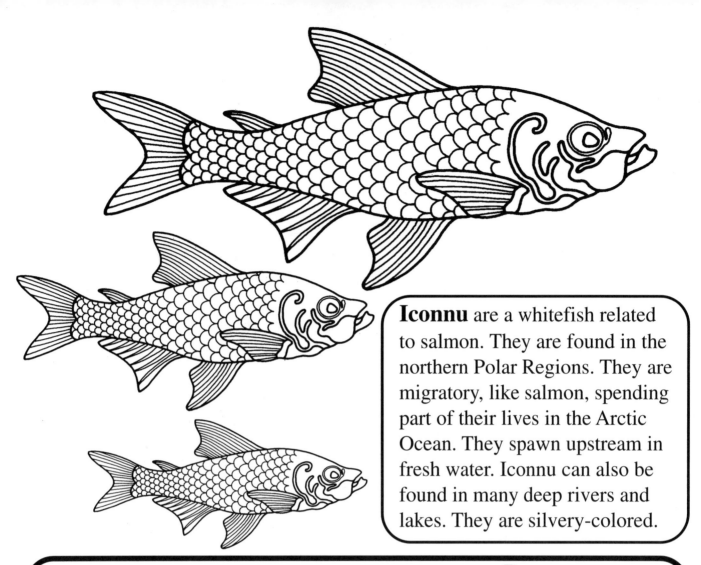

Iconnu are a whitefish related to salmon. They are found in the northern Polar Regions. They are migratory, like salmon, spending part of their lives in the Arctic Ocean. They spawn upstream in fresh water. Iconnu can also be found in many deep rivers and lakes. They are silvery-colored.

Isopods are small tan, green or brown crustaceans with hard exoskeletons. They can be found throughout the world, and live in both Polar Sea Regions. They are food for many species of fish and for certain whales that feed on the ocean bottom. They are found along the shorelines under rocks and in shallow waters among kelp.

J

Jellyfish of all varieties live in the Arctic and Antarctic waters. They float with the currents and are occasionally washed ashore by storms and high tides. Jellyfish tentacles contain hundreds of stinging cells, called nematocysts. These stinging cells contain tiny poison barbs that harpoon anything touching them. Jellyfish are most often transparent, but some are purple, yellow to orange, brown or white.

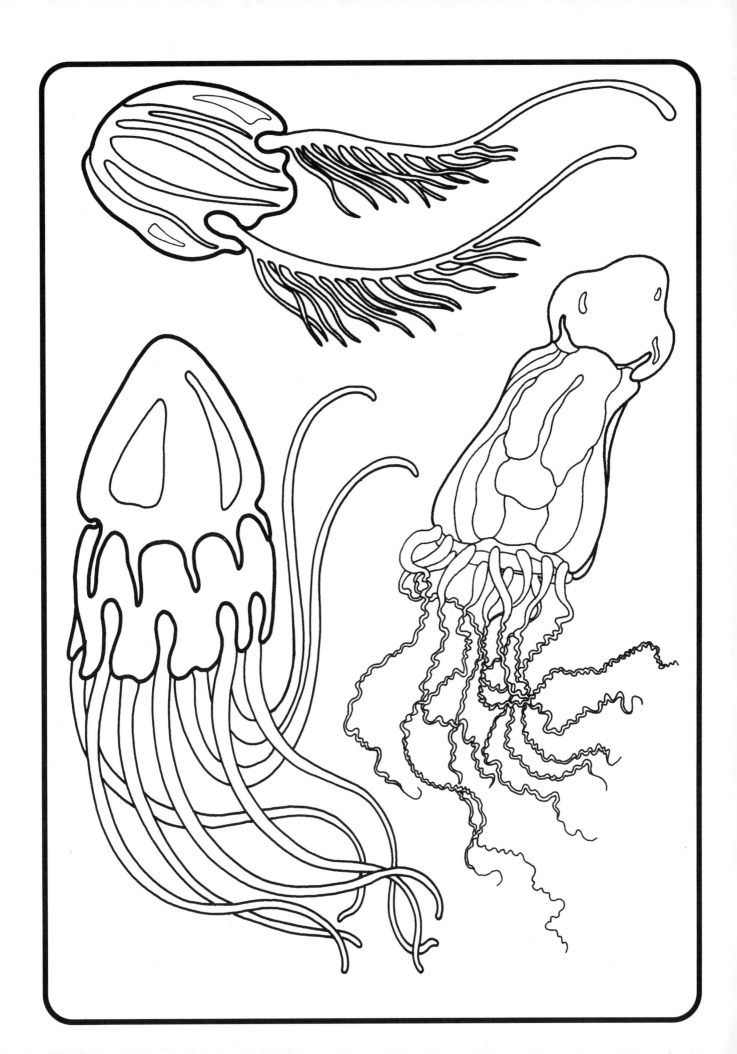

K

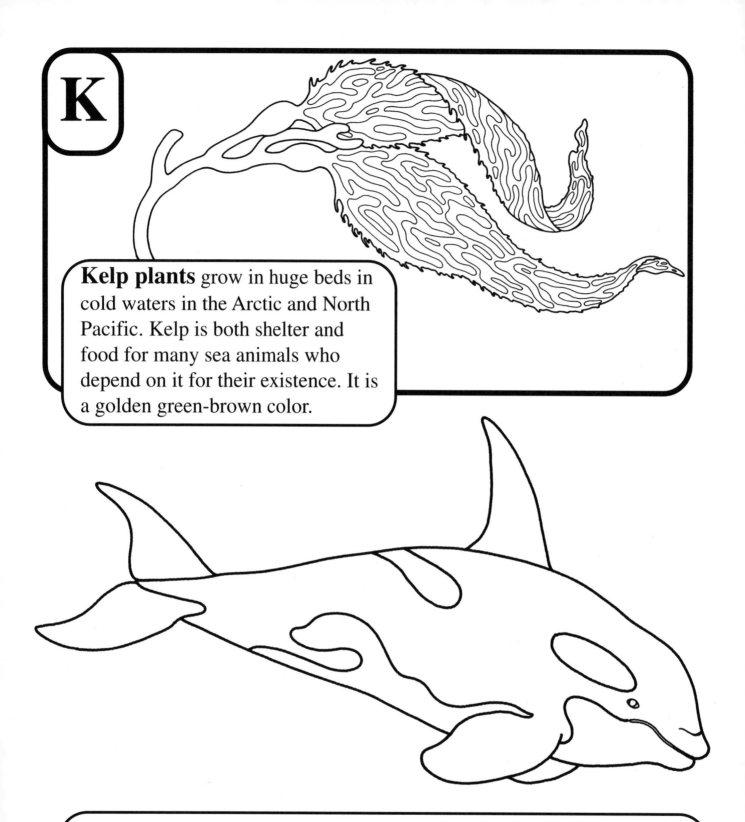

Kelp plants grow in huge beds in cold waters in the Arctic and North Pacific. Kelp is both shelter and food for many sea animals who depend on it for their existence. It is a golden green-brown color.

Killer whales, also called orcas, are actually large dolphins. They can grow to thirty-two feet in length and weigh as much as nine tons. They are found in all oceans, but prefer colder waters. Killer whales live in both Polar Regions, feeding on fish, penguins, seals and occasionally even larger whales. Killer whales are highly intelligent and social animals. They live in small family groups of up to thirty whales called pods. They are black, with white markings.

Krill are small two-to-four-inch-long shrimplike crustaceans found in the open ocean. Krill can be white or green, but are usually red. There are eighty-five different species of krill, eleven of which are found only in the Antarctic. Krill form dense swarms, feeding on microscopic planktonic algae. They are a principal food source for baleen whales and nearly all other animals that live in the Antarctic region.

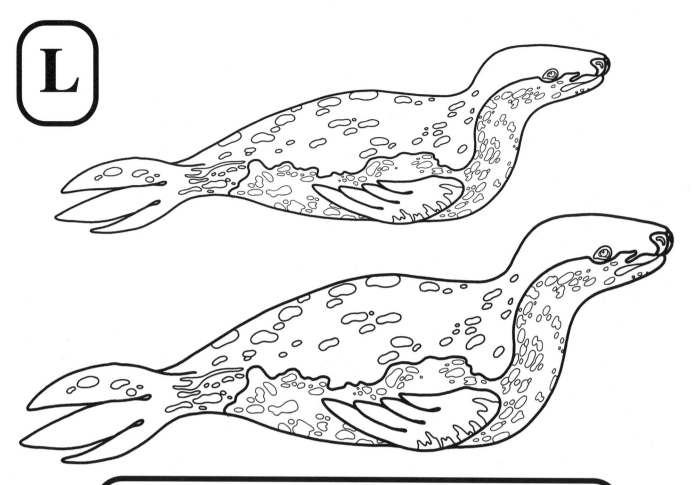

L

Leopard seals are ferocious predators, eating not only fish and krill but penguins and other seals as well. They are the largest of the Antarctic seals with large jaws and long necks. Leopard seals have a spotted gray-brown coat. They are usually solitary, but may occasionally haul out on ice near penguins or other seals. They are too clumsy to catch prey on land, but are extremely agile underwater.

Limpets are closely related to snails and abalones. When disturbed, they clamp down so tightly on a rock that they are difficult to pry off, even by the sea stars that prey on them. **Tortoise-shell limpets** are brown, blue or cream colored, and can be found in the Arctic.

Loons can be found breeding in the Arctic regions in summer. They forage in marshes and tidelands and along open coastlines. Birds in breeding plumage have a bold black-and-white pattern, with a silvery-gray neck and head. Loons spend most of their lives on or near water, and are adapted to an aquatic existence, with webbed feet and short wings. They are able to dive underwater without leaving even a single ripple behind them. They travel in large flocks, migrating south in the winter.

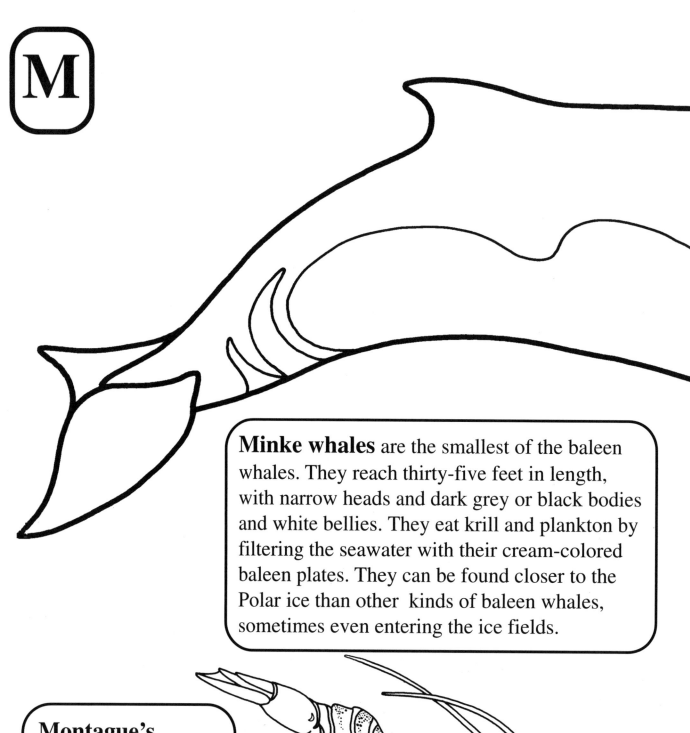

Minke whales are the smallest of the baleen whales. They reach thirty-five feet in length, with narrow heads and dark grey or black bodies and white bellies. They eat krill and plankton by filtering the seawater with their cream-colored baleen plates. They can be found closer to the Polar ice than other kinds of baleen whales, sometimes even entering the ice fields.

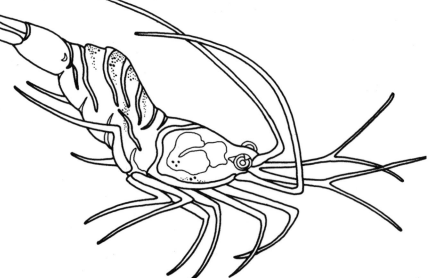

Montague's shrimp are found in the Arctic and south to Rhode Island in water up to 100 feet deep. They are pink or red, and three to four inches long. The larvae float in the ocean as plankton.

Mud stars are small sea stars, just two inches in diameter. Many types of sea stars are predators, but mud stars ingest mud, deriving nourishment from any organic particles they find in it. They are a pale yellow color or light brown, with brown tube feet. They live in soft mud on the sea floor in deep or shallow waters from the Arctic to North Carolina.

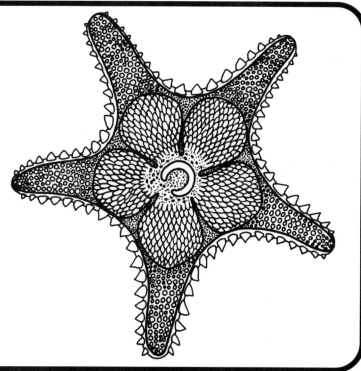

N **Narwhals** inhabit the Arctic near the ice pack, where they live even in the winter. Their favorite food are squid, which they pursue down to depths of 900 feet. Only the male narwhal has a tusk. It is actually a tooth growing out of the left side of the skull and can reach nine feet. The function of the tusk is unknown. It may be used to protect the narwhal's young from sharks. Groups of males have been seen jousting, perhaps battling with their tusks for dominance. Adult narwhals are dappled white and black and their young are a mottled gray-brown. They grow to fifteen feet long.

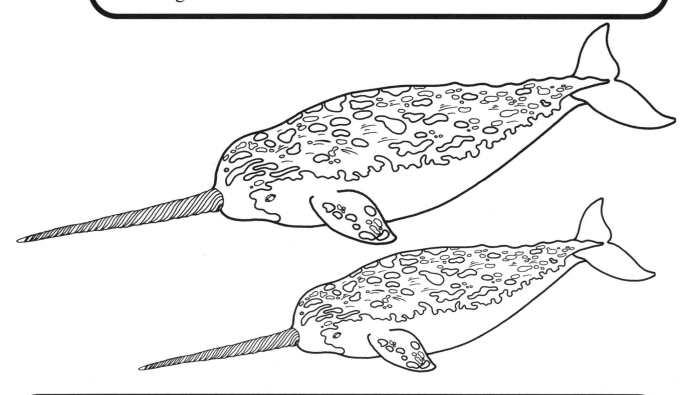

Nudibranchs are mollusks. They grow to between one and four inches long, and feed on sea anemones and hydroids. Some varieties incorporate the stinging cells from their prey into the appendages on their backs as a defense. Among the Arctic species, the **red-gilled nudibranch** has red appendages and a white body, and the **maned nudibranch** is white or brown with gray spots.

Northern bottlenosed whales spend the spring and summer around the edges of the Arctic ice pack, moving farther south in the winter. They grow to thirty feet in length and are tan or brown. Older males are usually a cream color and have a larger, more bulbous forehead. They are very inquisitive, readily approaching boats. Their numbers have been greatly reduced by hunting. They will not abandon an injured member of their pod, making them very vulnerable to whalers. There is a southern population of bottlenose whales found in the Antarctic region, very similar in looks and habits to the northern variety.

O

Octocoral grows even in the cold waters of the Arctic and Antarctic. It takes many different shapes. Some octocorals are red or orange with thick white stems. Others are white or pale yellow. At the end of each branch is a cluster of flowerlike polyps. At the center of each flower is a mouth surrounded by tentacles that capture plankton and food particles from the ocean water. The polyps can disappear into the stem when danger threatens.

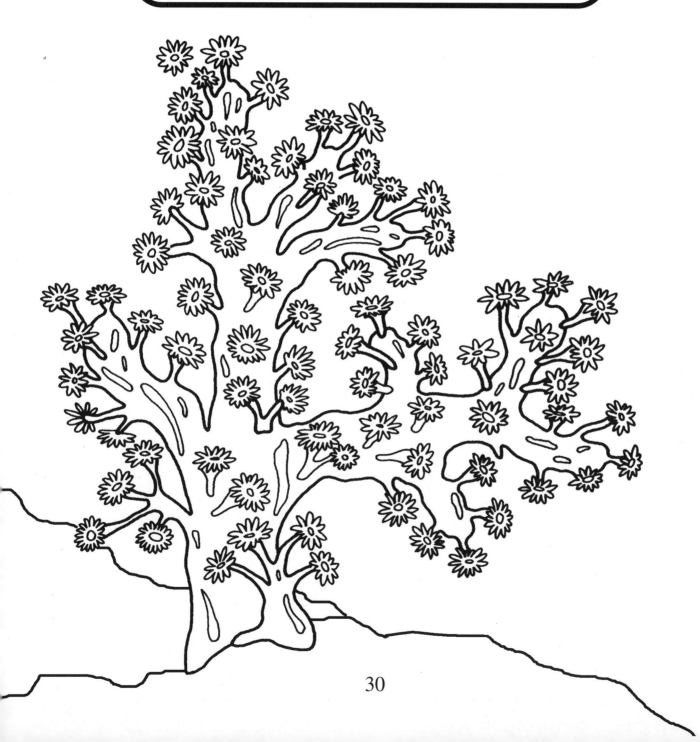

Octopus are mollusks, in the same family as snails. Octopus have keen eyesight, communicate with flashing skin colors, and have the most highly developed brain of any invertebrate. Experiments have shown they are able to learn and are quite intelligent. When in danger, they squirt dark purple ink into the water and make an escape. They hide in caves or shells, or even old bottles and cans. Octopus are grey or brown, with green and pink tones.

Ornate worms live in the sand or mud inside burrows, attached to the underside of a rock. The tentacles are yellow-orange, and the body is orange-pink. They feed by waving their tentacles in the currents.

P

Pelagic clam worms are predatory worms that grow up to six inches in length.
They live in sand or mud burrows under rocks.
They are red-brown, golden brown or green.
Worms are a common life form in the waters of both Polar regions.

Puffins live in the Arctic and North Atlantic, and nest on remote islands in burrows in the ground. They catch fish by diving, carrying as many as twenty fish at once in their beaks, and are skilled swimmers.
Puffins are black, with white cheeks and breast feathers. Their odd beaks are red, gradually becoming yellow near their faces, with a black triangle at the tip.

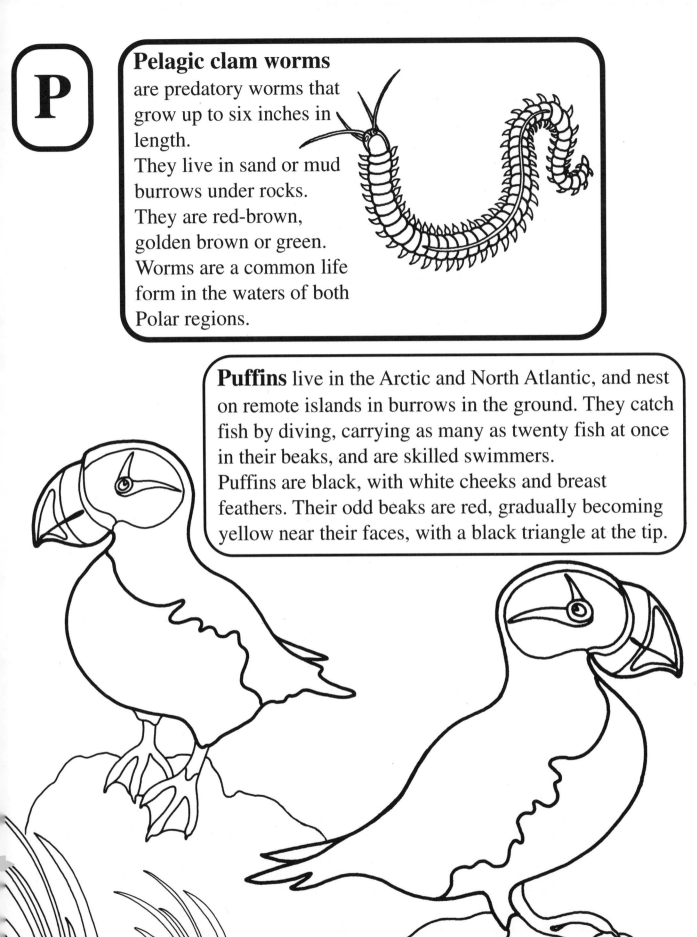

Periwinkles are sea snails that feed mainly on algae growing on rocks along the shore. **Rough periwinkles** can be found in the Arctic, and are yellow, gray, white or brown in color. They can be found high on the beaches, hiding in shady crevices. They seal themselves into their shells with their trap-door-like opercula to stay moist until the return of the water at high tide. They grow to about an inch long and one half-inch across.

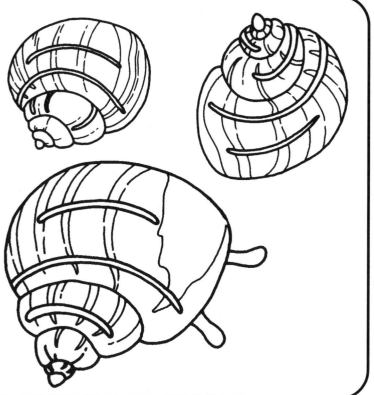

Q

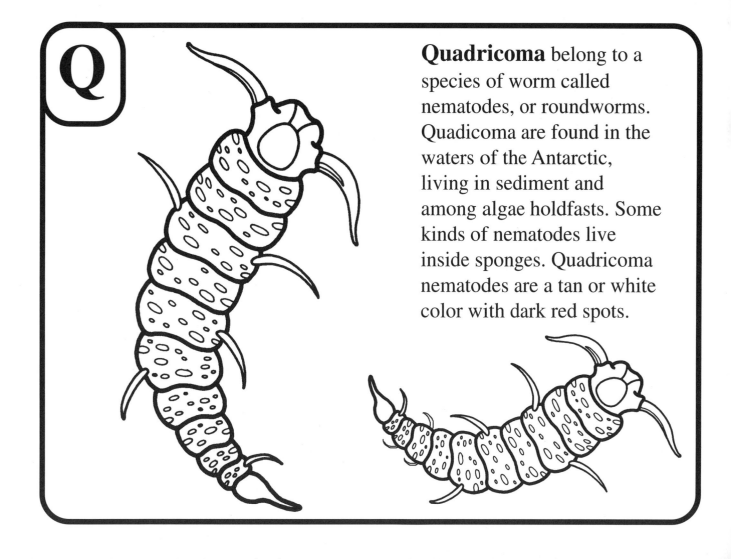

Quadricoma belong to a species of worm called nematodes, or roundworms. Quadicoma are found in the waters of the Antarctic, living in sediment and among algae holdfasts. Some kinds of nematodes live inside sponges. Quadricoma nematodes are a tan or white color with dark red spots.

R

Ribbon seals are an Arctic species of "true seals." They are less agile on land than eared seals, but they are better swimmers and can spend longer periods of time underwater. They live and breed in the Bering Sea on pack ice. They have a dark brown coat with white ribbon markings.

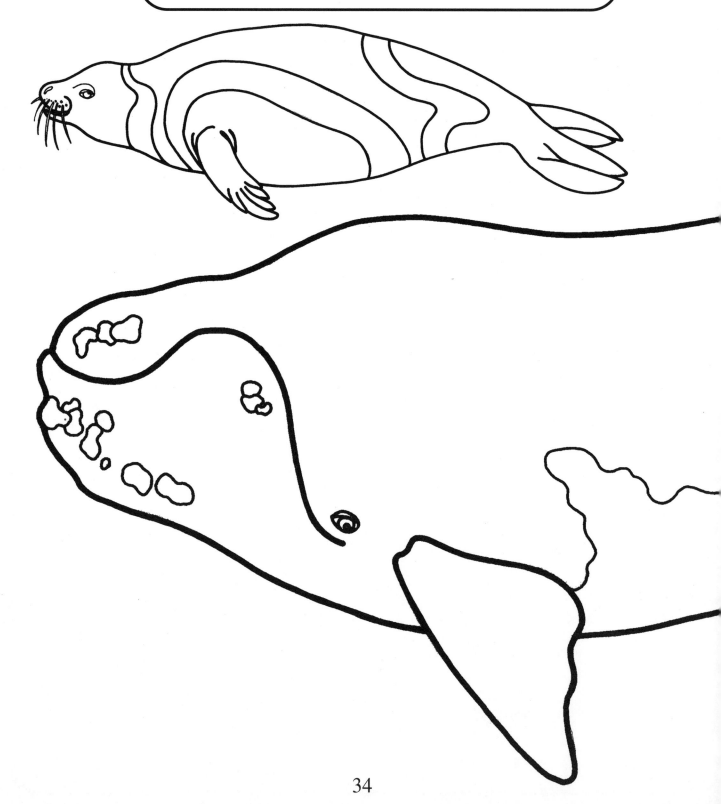

Right whales were hunted to the brink of extinction by whalers, who considered them the "right" whale to kill because they did not sink when dead. Right whales are slow swimmers, and are described as being playful and curious animals, qualities which made them easy prey. Right whale populations are making a very slow recovery. They have the unusual habit of raising their flukes into the air and using them like sails, letting the wind push them through the water. When fully grown, they are about fifty feet long and weigh seventy tons. They have dark brown or black skin, with white patches on their bellies. Their heads and jaws have patches called callosities. These growths vary from whale to whale in size and shape and are white or tan.

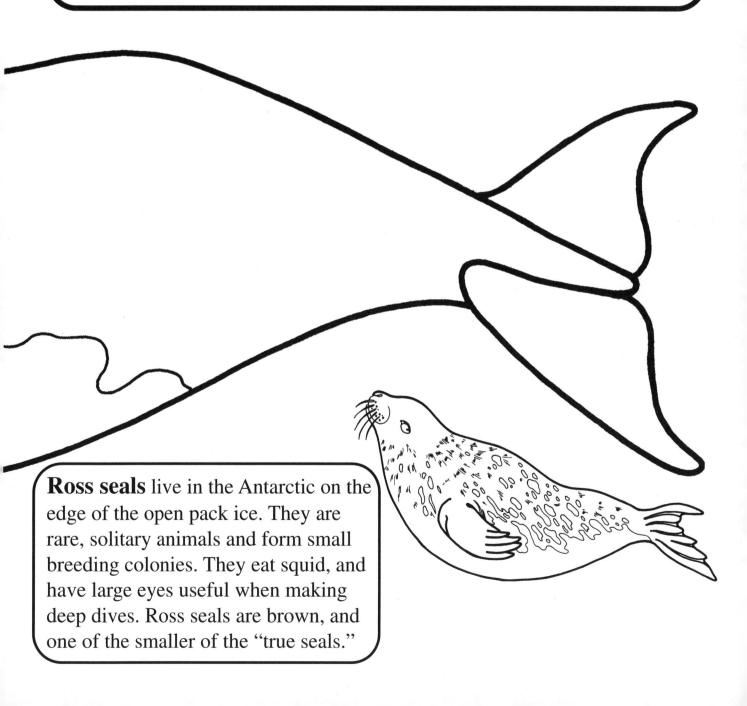

Ross seals live in the Antarctic on the edge of the open pack ice. They are rare, solitary animals and form small breeding colonies. They eat squid, and have large eyes useful when making deep dives. Ross seals are brown, and one of the smaller of the "true seals."

Sea otters live in kelp beds from northern California into the Arctic regions. Instead of the layer of fat that protects seals and whales from cold, sea otters' amazingly thick fur keeps them warm in the icy waters. They spend most of their time hunting for food, or grooming their fur. They groom constantly to maintain a layer of air bubbles in the hairs as insulation against the cold. Sea otters eat urchins, clams, snails, starfish and abalone. They are a keystone species in the kelp forests. By hunting urchins and starfish, which eat kelp, they help the kelpbeds to flourish. Sea otters are a rich brown color with lighter fur on their faces and black paws.

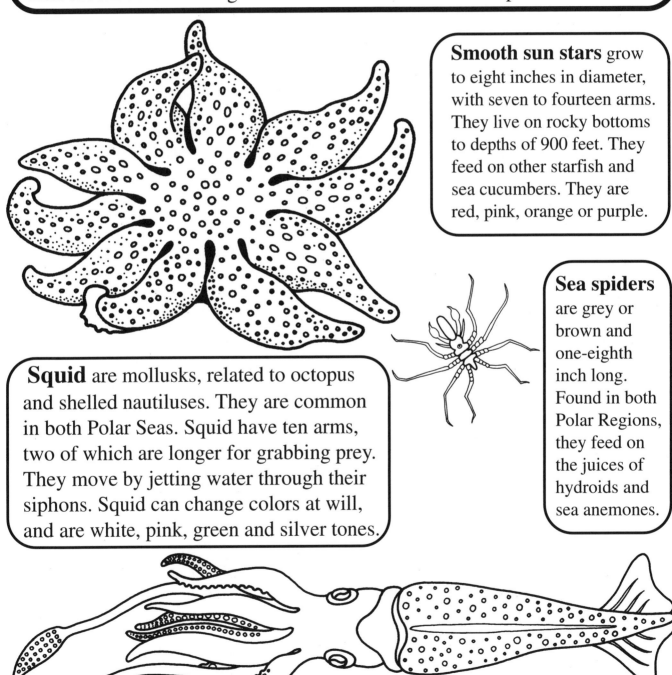

Smooth sun stars grow to eight inches in diameter, with seven to fourteen arms. They live on rocky bottoms to depths of 900 feet. They feed on other starfish and sea cucumbers. They are red, pink, orange or purple.

Sea spiders are grey or brown and one-eighth inch long. Found in both Polar Regions, they feed on the juices of hydroids and sea anemones.

Squid are mollusks, related to octopus and shelled nautiluses. They are common in both Polar Seas. Squid have ten arms, two of which are longer for grabbing prey. They move by jetting water through their siphons. Squid can change colors at will, and are white, pink, green and silver tones.

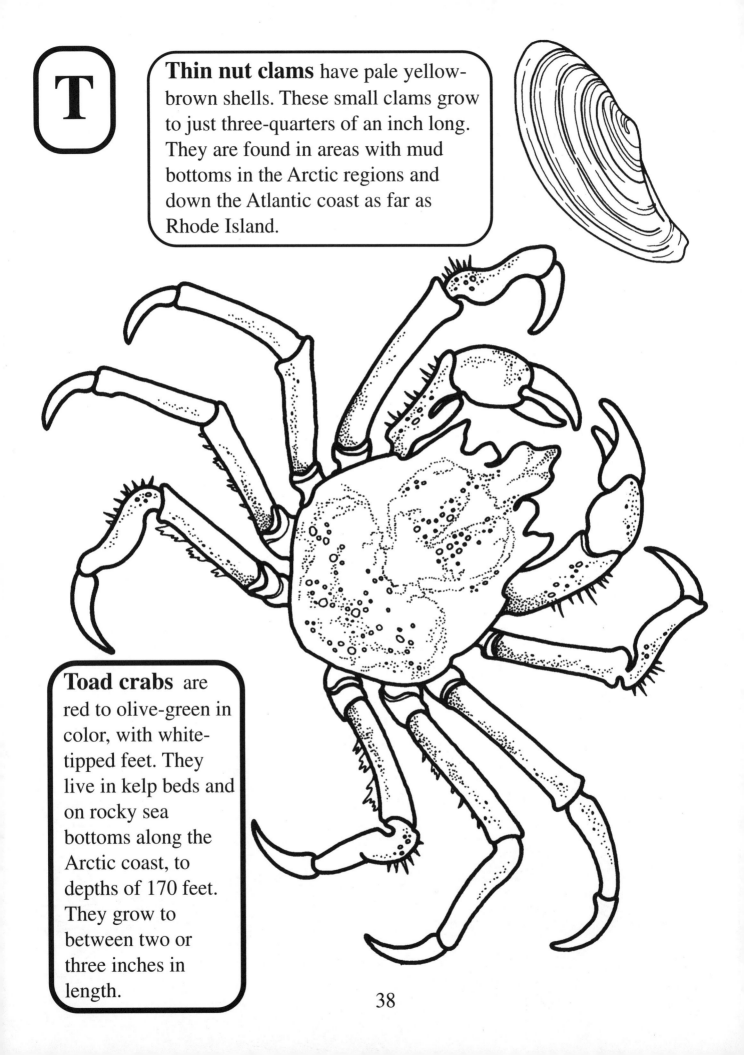

T

Thin nut clams have pale yellow-brown shells. These small clams grow to just three-quarters of an inch long. They are found in areas with mud bottoms in the Arctic regions and down the Atlantic coast as far as Rhode Island.

Toad crabs are red to olive-green in color, with white-tipped feet. They live in kelp beds and on rocky sea bottoms along the Arctic coast, to depths of 170 feet. They grow to between two or three inches in length.

38

Tunicates are also known as sea squirts, and are found in both Polar Regions. They live attached to rocks or kelp, and they pump ocean water through their siphon valves, filtering food particles from the water.

Sea peach tunicates are yellow-orange and red. They are fuzzy like peaches, and grow to five inches.

Stalked tunicates are orange to pink, and grow three inches tall. They can be found in very deep waters.

Sea grapes are small and translucent, with orange internal organs. They grow to less than an inch high and live in shallow waters. They brood their tadpole-like young inside their siphons.

Sea Peach Tunicate

Stalked Tunicate

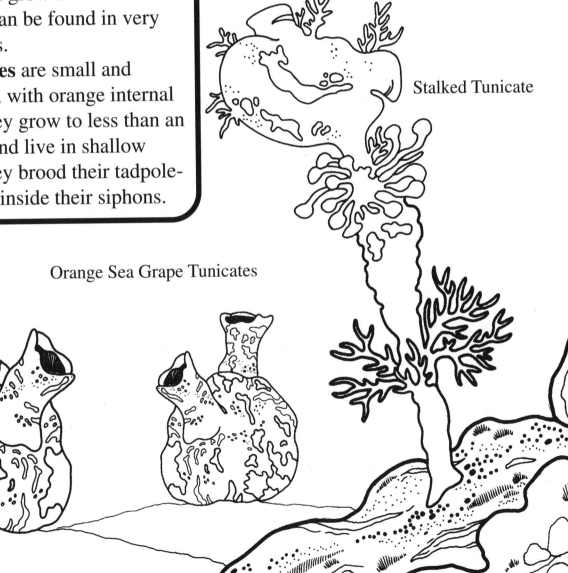

Orange Sea Grape Tunicates

U **Urchins** are related to sea stars and sand dollars. All belong to the phylum echinoderm. The green sea urchin is extremely abundant in Arctic waters. It can be found in large numbers on the sea floor around kelp beds, along rocky shorelines and out in deep water. The movable spines are the urchin's protection against predators and can rotate in any direction. With five rows of long, sucker-tipped tube feet they cling to rocks, gnawing their food with a drill-like tooth on the underside of their bodies. Some urchins actually drill into rock. Urchins are scavengers of the sea floor. They eat any debris they find, along with kelp, algae, sponges and corals.

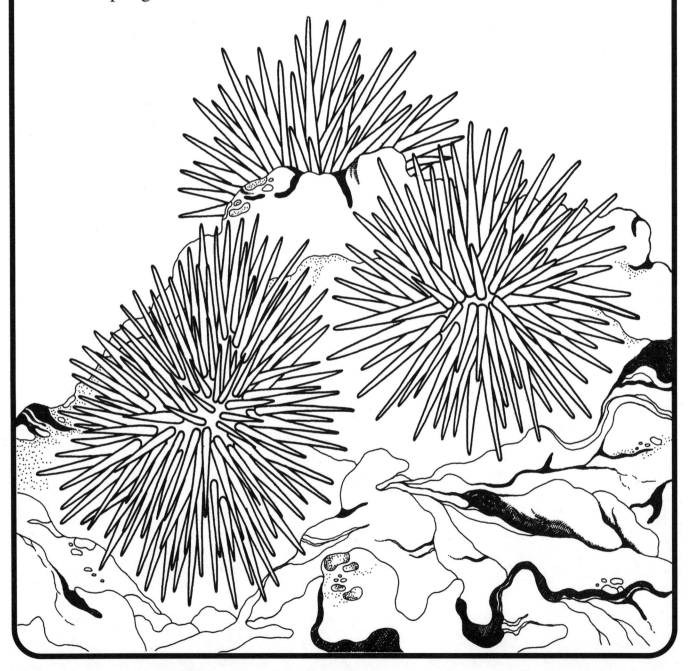

V

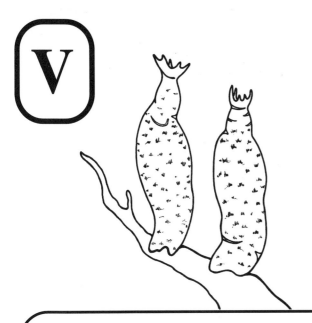

Vase tunicates are pale yellow or green. They grow up to six inches high. They can be found in protected harbors and bays in the Arctic and northern Pacific waters. Like other tunicates, they pump seawater through their siphons to filter it for microscopic organisms, which are captured by hair-like cilia and digested.

Vase sponges are just an inch tall. They are fuzzy, and a creamy yellow or tan color. They live in the Arctic, attached to rock, seaweed and shells. Sponges are very simple life forms, with no specialized internal organs.

Verrill's nemertean worms are long and slender and highly elastic. They can reach eighteen inches in length. They have orange heads, white bodies and purplish-red backs. They live in sandy mud, and entwined in the holdfasts of kelp. Verrill's nemerteans are found in Northern Pacific waters and around Alaska, but other nemertean species can be found in the waters of both Poles. Nemertean worms are predators of crustaceans and other worms.

41

W

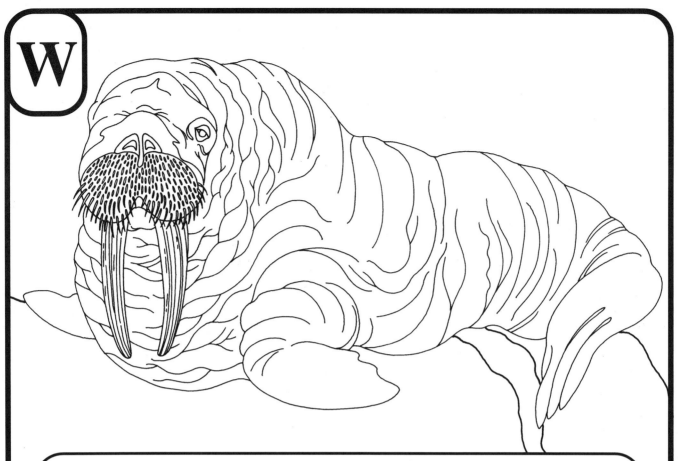

Walrus are like seals in many respects, but are unusual enough to be placed in a class of their own. They spend much of their time out of the Arctic water basking in the sun, but they have air sacs in their necks that can be inflated to keep their heads above water if they sleep at sea. They eat clams and shrimp, and glide on their tusks along the bottom while searching the mud for food. The tusks are also used like grappling hooks, to help the walrus pull itself out of the water. They are brown, and turn pink when the walrus sunbathe.

Waved whelks are snails found in the Arctic and further south. They grow to four inches in size, and are scavengers of the sea floor. They feed on any dead or dying fish or animal that hits the bottom. They can be found to depths of 600 feet. Their shells are grey, with hints of pink and yellow. The head and foot of the snail are black and white. The operculum, or trapdoor, is brown.

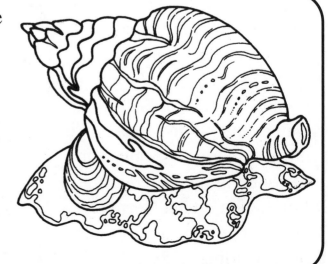

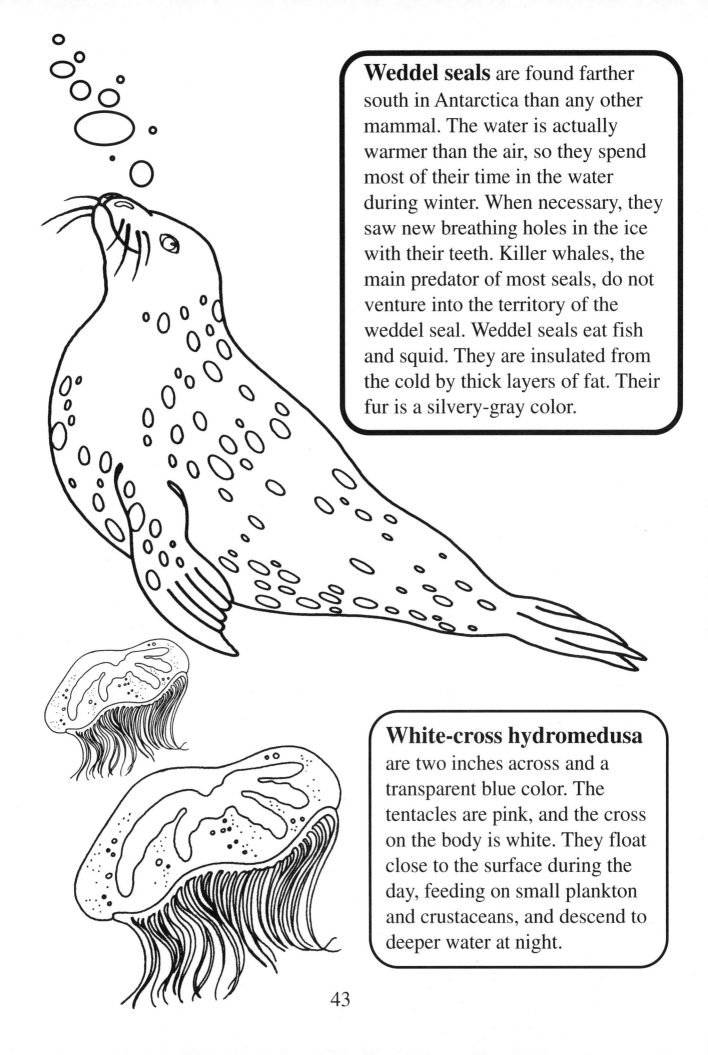

Weddel seals are found farther south in Antarctica than any other mammal. The water is actually warmer than the air, so they spend most of their time in the water during winter. When necessary, they saw new breathing holes in the ice with their teeth. Killer whales, the main predator of most seals, do not venture into the territory of the weddel seal. Weddel seals eat fish and squid. They are insulated from the cold by thick layers of fat. Their fur is a silvery-gray color.

White-cross hydromedusa are two inches across and a transparent blue color. The tentacles are pink, and the cross on the body is white. They float close to the surface during the day, feeding on small plankton and crustaceans, and descend to deeper water at night.

X

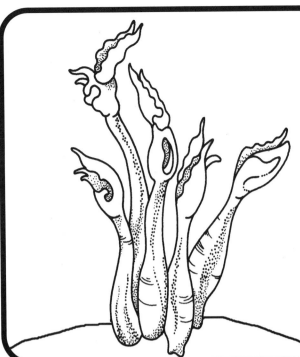

Xenobalanus barnacles are stalked barnacles that attach themselves to whales. They have been found on the flukes of the giant blue whale. They actually burrow into the skin, but are probably not noticed by the whale because they are so small. These barnacles are dark grey. "Xeno" means guest, or alien, and these barnacles are found mainly in the cold seas of the Polar Regions.

Xenocyttus are fish found in the waters of Antarctica. There are eight known species of xenocyttus fishes, ranging in size from three to ten inches. They are a silvery color, and live in deep water.

Xestospongia vanilla is a common encrusting white sponge that looks like cake frosting. It is sometimes edged with a pink color. It can be found along the Arctic coastline and south along the Pacific coastline.

Y

Yellow-nosed albatrosses are very shy, and tend to stay away from boats. The birds nest on the islands of Antarctica in September and October, on a mud cone nest on a ledge or in the shelter of vegetation. The eggs are white, with tiny red spots. In December the chicks hatch, and are ready to leave the nest by May. Yellow-nosed albatrosses eat fish, squid, shrimp and krill. They are sometimes seen in the north Atlantic. They are slim, elegant birds, with a yellow ridge on their beaks, white bodies, grey heads and black upper wings.

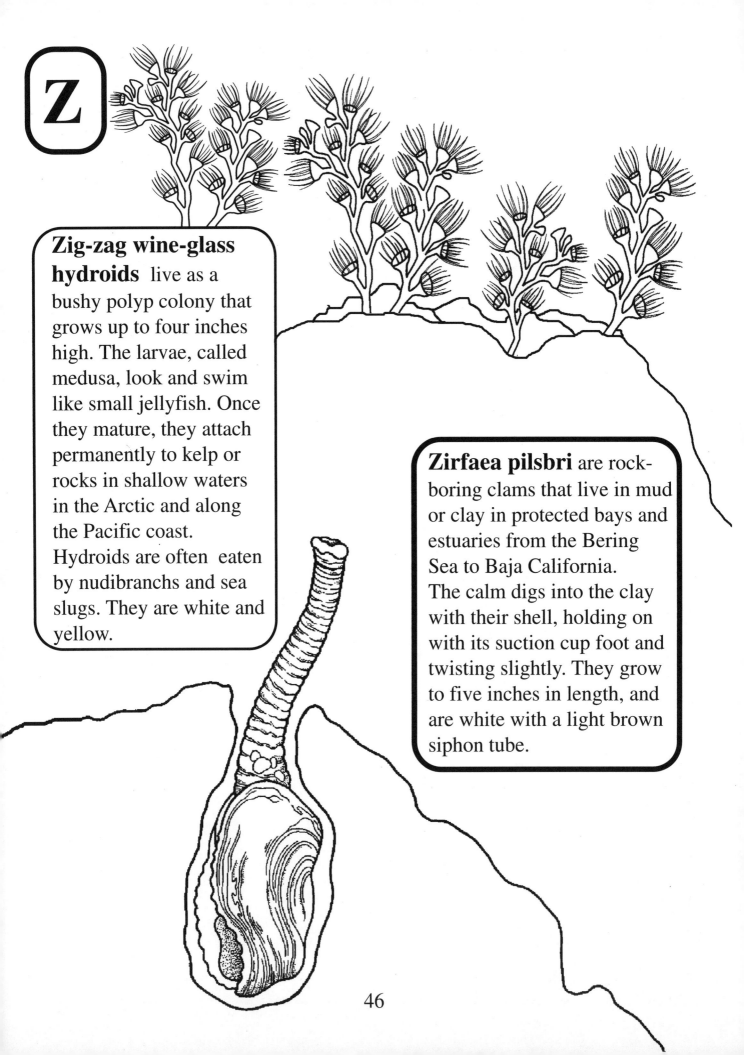

Z

Zig-zag wine-glass hydroids live as a bushy polyp colony that grows up to four inches high. The larvae, called medusa, look and swim like small jellyfish. Once they mature, they attach permanently to kelp or rocks in shallow waters in the Arctic and along the Pacific coast. Hydroids are often eaten by nudibranchs and sea slugs. They are white and yellow.

Zirfaea pilsbri are rock-boring clams that live in mud or clay in protected bays and estuaries from the Bering Sea to Baja California. The calm digs into the clay with their shell, holding on with its suction cup foot and twisting slightly. They grow to five inches in length, and are white with a light brown siphon tube.

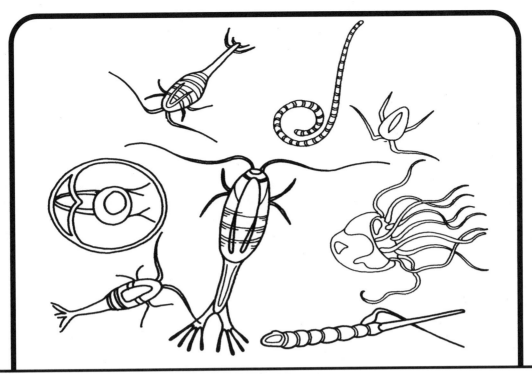

Zooplankton are tiny animals that swim or float in large masses in all the ocean's waters. Zooplankton are a vital part of the Polar Sea food chain. They are a primary source of food for krill, which in turn are fed upon by fish, birds, seals and whales. They are pink, brown, green and other colors.

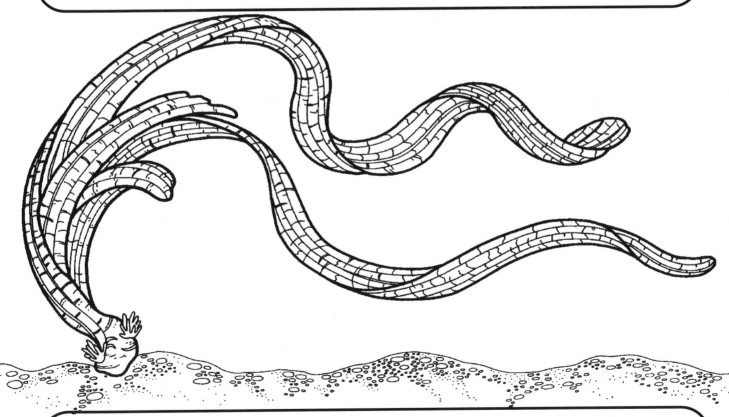

Zostera marina is a marine eel grass found in abundance in shallow waters in the Arctic. It forms dense beds in lagoons, where it provides important habitat for migrating birds and many other sea creatures. It is bright green.

Glossary

Arthropod   A large phylum of invertebrate animals that includes insects, spiders and crustaceans, distinguished by a hard exoskeleton and jointed legs and bodies

Baleen   Filtering plates in a whale's mouth that catch krill and plankton, while allowing water to escape

Bioluminescent   Glowing with a light produced by living organisms through a biochemical reaction

Bivalve   Animal with a pair of equal hinged shells held together by connecting ligaments

Bryozoan   A class of marine invertebrates that forms fixed, branching colonies, and reproduces by budding

Circumpolar   Surrounding an entire polar region

Crustacean   A large class of (mostly) marine arthropods with a hard outer skeleton and two pairs of antenna

Estuary   An area where the sea and a river converge and the water becomes brackish

Exoskeleton   The hard outer covering or shell that replaces an internal skeleton in arthropods

Holdfast   The roots of kelp or algae that attach the plant to rock or the seafloor

Hydroid   Invertebrate animals related to jellyfish, corals and anemones, that live as a fixed plant-like colony or as free-swimming medusa

Invertebrate   An animal without a spinal column

Isopod   Crustaceans with bodies composed of seven thoracic segments, each with a pair of legs

Medusa   The free-swimming larval stage of many kinds of fixed hydroids, resembling a jellyfish

Migration   Travel from one region or climate to another for feeding and/or breeding purposes

Mollusks   A large family of invertebrate animals including slugs, snails, nudibranchs, octopus and squid

Nematode   A class of worms living in soil or water, often parasitic in nature

Nudibranch   Colorful marine mollusks in the class Gastropoda, related to limpets, abalone and snails

Operculum   The hard plate, or door, that closes the opening of the shell when the snail is inside

Pack ice   Sea ice that forms when the water temperature drops below 28 degrees in winter

Pelagic   Referring to animals that live their entire lives out in the open sea

Plankton   Microscopic plants and animals that float near the surface of the water and are carried by the ocean's currents

Polyp   Animals with hollow tube bodies anchored at one end, and a central mouth surrounded by tentacles

Predator   An animal that kills and eats other animals in order to survive

Vertebrate   An animal with a spinal column

Zooplankton   A collective term for planktonic animals

Designed by Julia Pinkham
Composed in Times with Bongo Black display by Julia Pinkham
Printed on 75 lb Williamsburg Offset paper and bound by
BookCrafters, Fredericksburg, Virginia